"Timeless speaks to the juxtaposition between life's suffering and its beauty. Read these poems slowly, breathe after each line, and be taken to your depths, then ride up and out into life's beauty again. These poems will change anyone who reads them. Scott Hastie reminds us quite colorfully in Timeless that in both suffering and joy "nothing is ever ours to keep." A must read for anyone wanting to transform his or her life."

Jan Marquart, Literary Editor, USA.
Author of *The Mindful Writer, Still the Mind* and *Free the Pen*

TIMELESS

The best of Scott Hastie's
poetry from

1990 - 2020

Timeless by Scott Hastie
First published 2020
Centuria, London
Copyright © scott hastie
All rights reserved

ISBN: 9780992709358
e book ISBN: 9780992709365

A catalogue record for this book
is available from the British Library.

instagram scottie131313
twitter @scotthastiepoet
facebook.com/scotthastiespiritpoet

www.scotthastie.com

Source photo used for cover artwork is a shot of the night sky
during a Total Lunar Eclipse, over Brena Baja, on the east side of the island of
Las Palmas in the Canary Islands, taken by by Steve Bockling on 27th July 2018.

Dear Reader,

All the poems you will find in this, the first ever such compendium of my creative writing to date, were chosen to provide you with a personally informed and representative selection of the creative journey I have undertaken as a published writer and poet during these past thirty years.

More than anything, the narrative of this journey is one of thanks and gratitude for the many blessings that have thereby since come my way, ever since I first began 'chasing the light'.

For me, there was only ever one true ambition in life. From that charmed moment in the Pantheon in Rome, watching on as a beautifully elegant young woman walked reverentially across the marble floor of this extraordinary historic building to place a single red rose of the tomb of the painter Raphael. There and then, an insight immediately crystallized around a noble purpose for my life. Ever more certain that my task was now leave behind something true and beautiful, fashioned from my own life's experience that might have some chance of touching, moving and inspiring others, many years later. Surely, as an eager and idealistic young man, that was all I could ever hope for. And so, the die was cast!

Inevitably, there have been so many kindred spirits, along the way, to thank. Not least you, my readers… For, whoever you may be, wherever in the world you live… whatever your story… your age… your culture… your faith… thank you all so much for giving my writing your attention and granting it privileged access to your heart. Because, for me, that has been truly the most precious gift of all. Your on-going patronage succeeding as it has, in encouraging me to reach ever higher creatively, with each passing year.

Of course, there have been many other pivotal individuals, along the way. Not least my parents Jean and Peter Hastie who, in loving and raising me as best they could, were so instrumental in propelling me forward. Also, my lifelong and dearest friend the painter, Ian Stirling (sadly long since departed) to whom I also still owe so much. For it was he (and at a ridiculously young age too!) who first introduced me to all the great thinkers, artists and glorious creative souls that had ever lived. Insisting there should be no shame, nor ridicule to be endured by looking to learn from and be inspired by such luminaries.

My wife, Maureen has also been such a Godsend. What an angel she has truly been in my life. Ever since she first found me and rescued me from an albeit glamorously romantic state of loss and hollow despair! Moreover, what an extraordinarily loyal, singularly good and beautiful person she has proved to be, in choosing to stay faithfully by my side on this crazy journey, all these years. Together with all my amazing children and grandchildren too, each of whom have simply filled my life with such open joy, generosity and unconditional love. How on earth could I have ever stayed nourished and fuelled for all the challenges ahead, without this precious and on-going endowment of life's goodness? My friends, it simply would have not been possible…

And, as in the life stories of so many others before me, it is important to acknowledge a few other key individuals who have stepped in with such valuable contributions, along the way.

It was my High School French teacher, Robert Peel (sadly later to die tragically in a house fire, at a time when he still had a young family) who first filled my head with the soaring voices of Rimbaud, Baudelaire and Sartre and believed in me, when so many others didn't. Not least the Head of English who thought me to be an impossibly annoying and arrogant young man. Always looking to correct her and claiming to understand the Lakeland poets better than she ever did. Needless to say, at the time, she was right about all that youthful arrogance!

Only to be trumped by the Headmaster himself who told me, as an eighteen year old, I was simply wasting my time looking to claim a major literary scholarship, in competition with graduates from all over the country. This was a life-changing and fully funded five-year award to both study and qualify as a chartered librarian, that I went on to secure. So sincere thanks to that daunting and no doubt well-meaning individual for all the doubts he had about me. Which of course only spurred me on, ever more determined to prove myself. Such is life…

My final individual thank you has to go to David Lidgate, a wonderfully wise and gentle old soul. His formidable and enlightening monthly counsel, helping me get to where I need to be, has simply been invaluable for more than ten years now. How fortunate indeed was I to first bump into him up in the Altiplano, in the middle of nowhere in Peru, all those years ago! Again, such is life my friends.…

Anyway, I'm conscious I have probably indulged myself more than enough now, dear reader. So it only falls to me now to wish that you enjoy the following collection and to hope that some of the pieces within might make you smile knowingly and maybe even shed a tear or two, along the way.

With Best Wishes

Scott Hastie, October 2020

Splendour sleeps
In the thick still grey skies
Of a season's bleakness.

The steady muted glow of the sun,
Its sorry circle of gold
Highlighting the snow covered,
White-edged portrait
Of a winter's afternoon.

Inside the ashes of the fire
Burn red raw.
We talk
And your eyes dance
In patterns of pleasure before me.

Selected Poetry

"What it would be like
To be infants again."

And as we grow older
And more saturated
By experience,
Even the saddest among us
Cannot begin to know
Or remember
The quality of life
That was there once
For innocence to indulge in.

And so here we are,
My love and I,
Just doing our best.

Like sunny morning nudes
We sit together
Scheming happiness.

Selected Poetry

Those few that matter,
They carry their spirit
Before them,
Like a flame in flower
Within eyes
That share knowing sorrows,
That may seek sex
As a solace
For the suffering in life.

In their own way
They are special,
They cling to the wild beast
In their heads,
And ride it through
A dull, dim
Ordinary man's world
Where youth fattens
And desire leaks away.

Selected Poetry

To kiss the fruit
And caress the flower,
To taste without tarnishing
Humble nature's natural dower,
In this sweet pursuit
I shall place my frail body
Till death's timely hour,
And do so
With only breath remaining
To wish that
Amidst the winds of the world,
It will not shake nor cower
In the face of quiet eternity.

Selected Poetry

Within the golden riot
Of a flat freezing autumn
Coldness quite suddenly
Has its own specific final smell,
A smoky meld of musk and damp,
The smell of loss and completion.

And thus tomorrow
Is made anew,
Though every step forward
On the soft first frost of winter
Will seem like an agony of intrusion,
Like walking on sacred relics,
Or broken bone china
That might crack and spit at you
With its own sense of finish
Of perfection.

New Poetry

See how we still seek
Safe harbour
From the hollow pain
That seeps into souls,
Lost of joy.

We grasp
At what juices we can
To become part again
Of the very scent
Of some sudden truth,
That can in its intensity
Outlast the seasons,
The moods and the melancholy.

After all,
Even on a sodden autumn day,
The cruel thorn
Of a bedraggled pastel rose
Still has the polished jagged edge
That crimson blood could burst upon.

New Poetry

My heart seems so fragile
Near the edge of joy,
It quivers with a resonance
Of something not quite understood.

Yes, such ecstasies are mine,
But still too often
Bitter-sweet longings
Can escape from dreams
And persist like pain
To haunt even the calmest of days.

I am sad,
Like the hot dust on the streets,
And the music of fresh fallen leaves
Caught in a sliding summer breeze.

New Poetry

Every new day
Our childrens' joy
Is as fresh as roses,
Even the birds chatter at dawn.

Tomorrow will be sharp
And noisy,
Like the bright spotted
Splash of wild flowers
That freckle
The shaded tawny look
Of ancient meadows.

How stubborn life is,
It clings like silver in our souls.

New Poetry

Oh, to be wise enough
To milk the moments
When they come
And store them away
More carefully in my soul.

Another fragile casket of love
Has been spilt and broken,
Sweet liquors
Have trickled away forever.

And so where now
Are the fruits
Of such fine ecstasies?

Sometimes,
When I'm tired and empty,
I tear through my head,
Like some mad reaper,
Searching in vain for faces,
Fields, flowers,
Lovers that are no more.

How they still stain my heart.

New Poetry

Out there
In the fragile shadows
Beyond the self,
Lurks unimaginable power.

Energies that conspire
In the darkness
To offer you
A tantalising glimpse
Of another world.

Possibilities beyond dreams,
The scalding risks of magic
Beyond mortality
That cannot help but slip
Through your fingers
As soon as you reach for it's blessing.

Like the stale perfume
Of a tired romance
The searing light of morning
Asks unwelcome questions.

Fragile hopes
Soon blistered by daylight.

Meditations

If there's an ambition
Then it's to damage dullness.
To cause a tear, a slash,
Some rip in the surface of things.

Not damage for it's own sake,
But an attempt to sever connections,
To abandon convention, obligation.
To escape pattern.

To reach down within the wound
And grasp something of
The soft visceral truth beneath.

Here, illuminated at last,
Nestles the ruddy glint
Of spiritual certainty;
Sweet moments of passion and healing,
Of sensual release.

Meditations

Age gathers, colludes.
Cadences fade fitfully,
Seemingly before their time.

But there are echoes still,
Shapes we inherit,
We inhabit, we bequeath.

A life however bravely spent,
Will always be jagged,
Incomplete,
Never far away
From being enveloped in darkness.

Some may say,
Especially those
Who've known joy in life,
That this is not right.

I tell you clearly they are wrong.

So, just as a dancer
Might spin for you
An exact pirouette
And release themselves
In the perfect burst,
A lingering silhouette of energy,
Be content to love,
To dazzle in the light,
If only for moments…

And then be gone,
With gladness in your heart,
Before the creeping shadows
Claim too much your sadness at leaving.

Meditations

Marks are made.

Despite ourselves
We etch away,
We leave behind.

A few might even dare
To place something
Proudly on the landscape,
Just for its own sake,
Or so that afterwards
They might be spoken of
By strangers.

But, either way,
It matters not.
For when our souls
Are open
Connections occur.

And perhaps
There is a clue here,
A hint
Of something more fluid,
More oceanic.
A fugue state
That makes more sense
Of all this,
Our pattern, our purpose,
Our struggle to be serene...

Meditations

Graced
With the chance to be here,
Even if only fleetingly,
Embrace whatever comes your way
And, in so doing,
However enchanting
Any treasures you uncover
Might be,
Their loss should never be your concern.

In this matter
Make your heart your queen
And follow her as faithfully
And bravely as you are able,
Just as swelling fruit
Hurries towards its own sweetness,
Shine whilst you can,
Without fear,
For nothing is as inevitable
As it seems here.

No, not even the fissures
Of loss and decay
We are oft led to expect
In this temporal world.

For whilst we fuss and fudge
The lines we are given,
Above, below and all around us,
Lingers the energy
Of countless others
Who already know for sure,
Just as it was long, long ago,
When they first found themselves
Enraptured,
So it is for them, again and again...
And now with only a dark empty hollow,
A feeble space of earth left in between.

Such is true joy's absolute certainty,
Its slow-lit fuse that burns holes
In the shabby shroud of death forever.

Angel Voices

The day is done
And no one is immune,
It's true.

That sense of a voyage
Slips seamlessly past,
For there is a finite beginning
And end to everything.

And yet a sense of connection,
A bejewelled purpose too,
Like the child
Whose way ahead
You've already lit,
Or the lover you've yet to meet.

Many such moments
Come and go, as they must,
Melting away
Into the space we are given.

But what endures for me
Is a persistent resonance,
Some heady wish
For access again
To a sense of wonder
In the stream of things,
That, this time round,
It might just be possible
To keep in my heart
A little longer.

So tarry with me awhile
And we will see
What we can do
To tenderly explore
Beneath the frail shell
Of all we've since become.

Trusting that maybe within
Such smoothly sculpted casing,
And still delicately enclosed,
Might just lie the silky lustre
Of some lavish
And joyful communion,
Waiting for its chance
To grip and catch the light again.

Angel Voices

Lost puppies
We are no longer,
That's for sure...
Since all that's been and gone
And the very essence of you,
Left behind in so many hearts,
Is never forgotten.

And, on a day such as this,
When your world is calm,
Full of warm smiles,
And your soul is at last
Let off its string,
One cannot help but sense,
For certain,
That all the love inside you
Comes from the best of those
You've known and loved
And those who came
And went before you too...

Sweet darlings! Sweet youth!
All our hope and dreams
Derive from just that.

So, show me the wonder
Of all you've seen so far,
Stretch the day to its limit,
And let us have no guilt
Left to waste for dreaming still.

Angel Voices

A need for connection,
Attachment.
Drawn in, enchanted by
Resonances with nature
And the kinship of others,
With beauty
Forged by heart's endeavour.

And so should we
Always aspire to polish
Such precious attainment
With love,
A blessed friction of sorts
That allows us
To birth our night into day
And bathe it clean,
So that beloved things can glow
Together in a litter of light.

Angel Voices

Life collects,
Pools around you.

It paints its highlights.

Nothing there
You can destroy
Or begin again.

Calm in aquamarine beauty,
Barely a hint
Of surf's snowy trim.

Today the sea is out
But will come again.

For the moment,
On the beach,
My love and I,
Naked and blissful
As can be.

In the soft,
Sun baked sand
History
Between my toes.

Sense how
Even the smooth stones
Ache
With stories of their own
In the shuddering
Light of day.

Angel Voices

Needing love,
We squeeze what we can
From a fluid landscape
Of life and light,
Gifted to us
But for a moment
In the scheme of things.

Hope glistens,
Daring us to do
So much more.

And, at our best,
When least distracted
By the petty cares
Of the day,
We hunger for a constant,
To find a flow,
A warm, healing current
We can swim within.

One soul's journey
In search of a tipping point.
The possibility of honour,
The chance of grace in our lives.

Angel Voices

We are anything
But finite or alone!
After all, the petals of proof
Are here in our hearts,
Are they not?

And however deflated
We might sometimes be,
Either by our own frailties
Or the cruelty of others,
- Inviolate -
At the core of our being,
The very prism
Of sanctity and self remains.

And latent there,
The quick-silvered opportunity
Of redemption,
To become enchanted again.

Sublime moments refracted,
Even if only for seconds,
Caught forever in your soul.

Threads

Our lives
A long line of enquiry
Inevitably riddled with mistakes.

And hurting
As you may be now,
What a wonderful thing
It is not to be alone.

This ashen cloth
Won't ever quite
Leave me be either,
Living as I do on a prayer.

But, as my eyes lift again
To the world,
I can at least be with you.

Your body, your spirit
Healing like warm stones,
Sourcing
And soothing the exhaustion
In my soul,
So I can fall back skyward,
Safe in your arms,
And survive to dream again.

Threads

Here I am,
As if to confound myself,
Just as I ever was.

Seemingly little more
Than an excited dervish,
Forever chasing shadows,
Knowing that,
Come what may,
Beauty will continue
To throng around me,
Till I am no more.

What was it I never told you?
For isn't it true that,
Without fear,
We are capable of anything...

The smell of fresh rain,
Like gunpowder on the lawn,
Embellishes the day,
As the summer rips on.

And we can but wonder
As flawless
Early morning moisture,
Stranded on a leaf,
Glints in the sunshine.

The world watches
And waits for us, it seems...
As if to suggest 'tis best
To have an unquiet response
To the nature of things.

So drink deep of your sorrows,
Drink deep of your joy
And then love
And live restlessly
For as long
As the charged ache
In your spirit allows.

Threads

Despite what we imagine
In our sometime pain,
Beset
Either by aching anticipation
Or subsequent loss,
Lovers are never found by chance.

So tell that to the trees,
Who've seen it all
Countless times before
And can only stand apart
In the meadow of life
And wait
For us to dream again,
Like some broken hearted waif
On a grimy street,
For whom only the predatory
Are likely to stop.

For not even fool's comfort
Can cling on there
To inhibit notes of caution
That would otherwise
Trim our wings,
Spoil any such dividend.

And so much more too!
Seems like
We always had this coming.
Our needs, till met,
Like rising sap,
Like clotted pollen in the air.

As it always is
In beauty's sweet surrender,
Desire is the irresistible pull
That draws us steadily
Onto one another
And then fruits.

You were in me all along.

Threads

There is an intricate chain
At work here,
From one fleeting moment
Of grace to another.
A myriad of links,
Far too long and interlaced,
Even within one
Tentative soul's journey,
To fathom.

And so the challenge
Is a simple one,
To keep bringing light to bear.
And to do so
With all the good faith
One can muster,
Till some chinks appear.

A fateful knock at your door
That will surely come again.
And the choice then
Will always be a stark one,
Between surrender of sorts,
Or recourse to hollow dreams,
Long since eclipsed by time.

Our conjoined instincts,
Like sexual fire,
Come and go.
But that's the way of things.

Forever in the background
A persistent, elemental energy
That didn't ask to be here,
Just is...
And when it bursts forth
'Tis a wonderfully furious thing.

Threads

As we toil and spin,
Pause and gather in the stillness,
Whenever you are able.

Trusting that,
Time after time,
This might bind ever deeper
In your soul
And, one day,
Come gloriously to bear.

Otherwise how vain
A deceit
Is such constant distraction,
That leaks into everything
To spoil our chances.

And, in so doing,
Look how we fashion instead
A raw and unnecessarily restless
Sadness in our hearts.

For it is what it is,
This life,
No more and no less...
And everyday
It shines upon us
With a patience
That is inestimable.

So take heart from this
And simply surrender in moments,
As best you can,
Even if only in modest ripples
That gently caress
The shore of your dreams.

Threads

Disturbed as we are
By greed and vanity,
All the while
There is so much else
Here for us,
An abundance of triggers
Into both light and depth.

Far beyond
The gentle balm of faith
And the comfort that brings,
A huge and unimaginable love,
An iridescent vignette
Of sheer beauty.

And, slowly but surely,
We are being pulled in,
As one episode
Follows another
On our transit.

Gradually becoming wedded
To something.
The purple light of divinity
That we call God.

As, step by step,
In trying to understand love,
We become fearless.

Bold fires
Within us now
The run of many waters
Cannot quench.

Threads

The heavy weight of history
Directly abuts
The promise of tomorrow.

Come what may though,
Even spears, as they will...
I cannot help
But be laid bare.

For mine's a quest,
As yet unabandoned,
To be pure.

And all the while,
Being led that way too,
While the rarest of promises
Still cavort in my soul.

Just as it was at
The very beginning,
Whether pierced by joy
Or fear,
My own wounds to date
Focal points of emotion,
Now glowing red raw again.

Enduring transmissions,
Without which
One would surely have to
Start over again,
Without any narrative of hope,
Nor glimpse of heaven
Or twist of pain.

Threads

Inside every single,
Obdurate,
Intractable skull
Is an entire universe
Humming,
Every bit as vast
As the heavens above,
From whence we all came.

Albeit that we remain bound
To a narrative
That sometimes needs
To remind us
Of our mortality,
And in so doing,
Will punish and wound,
Seemingly without care
Or remorse.

But be not afeared.
Wear any such scars well,
Knowing that,
For every moment
Of suffering,
Others will arrive
That will instead
Pierce you with joy.

Open the doors
Of your heart
And they will come.

And for every cruel arrow,
Sweet caresses of delirium
To nourish your soul.

Threads

Treasured energies
Can evaporate like steam,
When hot meets cold...

And so, my hands
Are gathered together
Before me,
As if to hold
What is precious within.

To make of myself
Sweet sanctuary,
Sensing
What inspired quivers
Remain
Still seem
Too beautiful to die.

Slip away though
They must.

But for nought,
Have I whispered
To my past,
Can I begin again?

For such is the illusion.
Nothing is ever
Ours to keep,
Rather only to glory in
For a while,
Nourished
By brilliant residues,
Till blest again.

This then our lot.
As, step by step,
Faith accrues.

Threads

Whenever you can conjure
The stillness to notice,
There is
A sense of the ancient
Hanging in the air.

A lingering spiritual fragrance,
Full of knowing,
That dresses
Contemporary journeys
Like ours.

And always set against
Such a broad tapestry,
Long woven too
With telling details
That confirm who we are,
Albeit still as raw
And naive as any infant.

All the more so
When stood, toe to toe,
With the luminosity
Of days gone by.
And embarking,
As best we can,
On the benevolent
Opportunity
Of one thin slice
Of a chosen life,
However glorious,
Or loaded with pathos
This eventually becomes.

No chance of tragedy
Here though!
For we truly are,
As we come to recognise
Ourselves to be,
Mere receptacles.

Gilded chariots
That our spirits ride out,
But for a hallowed moment in time.

The merest splash of presence
In the serried halls of wonder.

Threads

If you listen carefully
There's a constant purr
In your soul,
With ambitions
Of provoking a response.
Akin to a mother
Forever nudging
Her fledglings forward
Into the light.

And this is reassuring,
As it's meant to be,
Putting the lie
To insignificance
Being the essence
Of our existence,
When the truth
Is quite to the contrary.

All this a gift
Easy to accept,
When such benevolence
Holds so steady,
Just waiting to be noticed,
Like the soft sigh
Of a tender young tree
In the gentlest
Of summer breezes.

Pranic Poetry

A sheen, a glow,
A charisma of sorts.

All we've come to know,
To touch the essence of,
Leaving behind a memory,
A presence of its own.

Energies
That eventually settle,
Coming to rest somehow
In the very fabric
Of who we are.

I see this so clearly
In the eyes of others.

Every moment
That has gone before
Bringing us here,
My friend.

And yet with so much
Still left to absorb.

Joy and pain
Spread so evenly
Along time's heavy arch.

Pranic Poetry

To live a little
You have to die a little,
So says the angel's
Enigmatic smile.

Never was the need
For any anvil of angst
Upon which
To crack open
The coded chronicles
Of such a pointed
Lifetime dilemma.

Till then, limited
By such dominant
Conviction
That fears the end so.

And such
Are all our hopes,
Freer to flower
Brighter still
When no longer clad thus.

Every true passion
Shared since
Speaking so clearly to this,
The resolute onward journey
Of our soul.

Pranic Poetry

We are all prophets
Of our own existence
Are we not?

And come what may,
'Tis always
Such noble ambition
To leave telling traces
Of ourselves
Wherever we can.

Thus do all our lives
Become
An enduring tapestry
Of pointed moments,
Albeit seeded with loss,
The ache of which will pass
Whilst such sweet emotion
Remains.

See how potently
That narrative runs on!

And to guide us on our way,
Amidst the endless sway
Of needs and desire,
Delicate patterns made,
Filigrees of real meaning.

The absolute truth
Of raw emotions
Etched on our heart,
Left behind,
Radiant,
As pathways to tomorrow.

Pranic Poetry

An old view
Seen anew.

Lost
In morning perfection,
The illusion
Peacefulness
Improves everything,
When fervour's a resource
Used all too sparingly
And there's
So much wonder
Out there
To even ruffle the surface of.

How often
Do we turn away though?
Timid, as we are.

And without such sparks
Time can pass by,
Like an empty whisper,
Meaningless and negligent.

Till, all at once,
There you have it,
Pulsing within you,
The day of days!

Whatever else
Might come your way,
This you will always know.

Never rewarded thus
Unless you sing so.

Pranic Poetry

In a world
That is far from certain,
This is for all lovers
Still to set forth,
Or imagining
They've yet to arrive.

This fitful journey
Of ours
No sideshow,
Albeit part
Of an ingenious conceit
That draws us tenderly
Towards the light,
Where chances
Can be so sweet
And every joyous release
Cannot help
But seed another.

So here it is!
And there
It ever was too,
Oh, but we knew it then.

Such sublime mapping,
The code of tomorrow
Already built into
All our yesterdays.

Pranic Poetry

Somewhere
There's never a sigh,
The choicest of gifts
Are always given,
Never chosen.

Our precious being
So much more
Than a vessel to fill,
When the world
Is so awash
With opportunity.

So dare to ignite
Fires of joy
Wherever you are,
Even if all
You might then
Be tempted to wish
Could well
Be yours forever,
Will one day
Be lost to you
In a changing of the light.

One in, one out,
It's a rum do!

Along with the fear
Of being forsaken
Or forgotten.

This will never happen
To a generous heart.

Pranic Poetry

Like the curiously
Regal stance
Of a proud young deer,
Surveying
The early morning mists,
At any given moment
I am an aggregate,
The absolute sum of all
That has gone before.

And even
When I'm no more,
I will remain still
In every facet of place,
Of presence, of purpose,
Of breath
And bare beings too,
Any of which
And each of whom,
Would never have been
Quite as they are
Destined to be now
Had I not come
To settle here
Awhile too.

So well before the time
To slip away
Gathers much pace,
So should we all
Endeavour to love,
To leave
The best of ourselves behind.

And forever remember
The need to be kind.

Or else, who knows
What quiet despair
Might otherwise live on
In the still beating hearts
Of others.

Pranic Poetry

What is this life?
If it is not
As if to walk
Weightless
In this thin, bright air.

Openly and lightly
Like children
You know...

Simple joys,
Easily found,
That resonate
Beyond all measure.

Thus are we ushered
Gently into this world
And then challenged
To find our way home again
With our hearts open,
To where heaven knows
There are pearls awaiting.

Along with the chance,
Day by gleaming day,
To come to realise
The more generously
We shine,
The more we will
Blossom and prosper
Along a path
Where how stunning
It is to still be alive
When, just once in a while,
Those who could never sing
Suddenly can!

And as you pause
To marvel at that,
Best to know all those
Who similarly bless you
In faith
Helped make it so.

See how boundless love
Brings time to its knees.
A gift beyond compare.

Pranic Poetry

See how,
Around
The stream's
Silvery edge,
Reflected light
Dances on the surface
Of rushing water.

Becoming
The very essence
Of life
And motion itself,
Effortlessly tapping
Into timeless truths
That, once absorbed,
Echo right back
At you
More than ever before.

And with a peerless
Reminder
That's both soothing
And humbling
Of how,
In a single lifetime,
One could never oneself
Accumulate
Such knowing grace,
Gather up such melody,
Nor offer such endless
Nourishment.

Still here
With the chance
Of some
Sweet release though.

And, for so many
Amongst us,
Would that it were so!

To dream
That one day
Within
Such a river might flow.

Pranic Poetry

Like some flutter
Of a fishing line,
Whose glistening hook
You've already
Been caught upon,
Don't ever look to
Undervalue suffering
When it comes to visit.

Equal as it is
To any kinder, softer,
Sweeter experience.

For, taken altogether,
This is how
We are nourished,
How we grow into
The glorious spaces
In between,
Till some vital sense
Of mystery
Is at last dissolved,
The sun glints again
Through the forest
And our hearts are captured
In a blaze of joy
And aching melancholy,
Like a memory of heaven.

From that moment on,
We become seekers.

And how often then
Do we lay down
To make beauty.
Only to let it all go again
Longingly,
Trusting that these,
Our devotions,
Will somehow always endure.

See how boundless love
Brings time to its knees.
A gift beyond compare.

Pranic Poetry

*With an acknowledgement
to Peter Matthiessen*

Sometime bruised
By the very air I breathe,
In the ceaseless
Crush of life,
When all that has been,
And will be no more,
Dallies still.

And truly
Moving forward
Can seem
Like a never ending
Series of encounters
With the intangible,
Too often
Just out of reach.

There comes a prayer
In my heart
As if to usher me
Affectionately
Towards a finer state
Of being,
Far beyond all notions
Of self doubt.

And then, Yes!
I see that you are here.

As if to hold my hand,
Cushion a tear,
Nurture my hopes,
Allay my fear.

How wonderful that,
Come what may,
Your timeless presence
Hovers so loyally
Over me still,
Like the loss
Of a sweet romance
Just waiting,
Oh so patiently,
To be rekindled.

Your beguiling smiles
And knowing laughter too!
The sweetest and most loving
Of reminders
That, for all the joy
And sorrows
I've bled and yearned for,
Soaked in equal measure,
How blessed am I
These days to be thus.

When so many
Poor souls
Amongst us
Lead such lives
Of quiet desperation
And die with their song
Still unsung inside them.

Pranic Poetry

Almost unnoticed,
Honey on my lips.

Everyday anew
In the clean,
Sharp air,
The fresh dew of morning.

A profusion
Of life's finer nuances
Only just
Beginning again
To slip
Their welcoming fingers
Gently through my soul.

Highlighting times
When all thoughts
Of past,
Present and future
Begin to overlap
And any shadows made
Simply fall to the ground,
Only to dissolve
Into dancing leaves,
Soon lost
On a joyous breeze.

'Tis the same
For everyone of us,
My friend,
Seeker or not.

And whatever
Iron-clad hesitation
May well still
Be loitering
Heavily in your heart,
One day
We will all achieve release.

Making this,
The final leg
Of our journey,
To where much lighter,
And far softer,
Sumptuous answers
Lie within.

Till then,
With each moment
Of elevation
Such as this,
Tantalisingly close.

Pranic Poetry

Look deep
Into your own self,
As life,
Its challenges,
Its gentleness too,
Runs its course
Kindly
Through your
Many chequered spirit.

And therein
Catch sight
Of something
Seemingly infinite,
A kaleidoscope
Of blossoming feelings
And emotion.

Recalling
After the event,
As we are always
Mysteriously
Able to do,
Just how
Such sudden despair,
Or indeed delight,
Can sometime
Creep upon us
Like twilight.

Often arriving
With such delicacy
We might not,
At first, even notice.

Conscious,
As we are,
That if we weren't,
From time to time,
So troubled,
So tested, so fallen,
We wouldn't be
Mortal at all!

Forever hankering
After sweet relief.
Such is devotion,
Love, compassion.

And realising this,
See how we come
Much closer than ever
From being just
One step away
From Earth's great gains.

A first glimpse of
The infinite garden within.

Pranic Poetry

See how our spirits
Ebb and flow...

And with a primal energy
That fuels
These seasons of change,
The very seasons of beauty.

As ever then,
The temptation is
Not to tend your garden
Carefully enough.

Though once gold,
Always golden...

For what is life
If it is not this?

The moment
When you first catch
A glimpse
Of your better self
In the tender eyes of another.

And as for you my darling,
Cling on tight
To this very same light
And the angels
Will still come
To find you,
To save you,
To make you anew.

In turn, arriving first
As a gently
Gathering whisper.
And then,
If fully welcomed in,
Soon becoming
More like the glorious swell
Of some magnificent orchestra
Whose sole ambition
Is to stir your very soul.
And, yes indeed...
To remind you
You too have known love.

Pranic Poetry

How blessed are we
To be for a while
In this,
The natural world,
Albeit
With its every whim,
Its necessary flux.

All the more so,
When no rule exists
That can even begin
To measure the scale
Of shift
In spirit required
To make
The very best of this,
Our passage here.

I can still remember how,
When the time came,
My own mother
And indeed hers too
Took their leave
So gently, so peacefully.
A beautiful softness there...

As if to remind us
It falls to us now
To keep the faith,
To carry on giving
As joyously,
As selflessly as we can,
No matter
How many stars
Have fallen from the sky.

Warmed
By something approaching
Our capacity for wonder
In the hope they still inspire.

Oh! To have such chances still.

Pranic Poetry

Time is forever short,
When your world
Can turn in a second.

And everything,
Frail or not,
Be irreversibly
Swept away.

Yet, all the while,
Moistened
By a gaze
That's like
A soothing balm
To any such outcome,
We cannot help,
But reach
For authenticity,
For purpose,
For meaning.

Fermenting
An unending aspiration
To make the world
Anew.

In itself,
A rebellion
Against waste.

After all,
From the soiled earth
Fresh flowerings
Will come.

And in their
Glorious wake,
A re-energised belief
In redemption,
True beauty.

Life seen afresh
In iridescent
Colours of promise,
Long since hewn
From an abandoned sky.

Pranic Poetry

When I am
As I am,
My beliefs
Gather in strength
Like swathes
Of glorious flowers,
With delicate veins of iron.

But when I am not.
And far closer
Instead
To a tarnished apathy,
That forever smolders
Under glutinous
Layers of time,
What a poor servant
To life,
A minion of misery
I become.

My muted cries
For solace
Progressively
Compacted
Like layers of
Atrophied rock,
Hope long gone.

Better then
That my spirit
Remains fluid
And supple enough
To yearn for
Fresh experience.

This a story
I've been told to tell you.

And it's one of triumph,
With an eternal narrative
Of real worth
That is forever playing out.

After all, my friend,
Who are we anyway?
If not the extraordinary
Unearthed from the dross.

Pranic Poetry

Here we are,
At times
Almost haunted,
It seems.

Underpinned
By a faith, a feeling,
A connection.
But to what?

An inbuilt tryst,
The irreducible
Essence
Of something
So vibrant,
Yet so illusive.

Especially
When you look
To clasp on tight
And claim it
As your own.

This the honeyed milk
That carries
The gift of a day.

A debt
We can never
Pay back,
Only acknowledge.

And, in living joyfully
And generously,
Honour as best we can.

All the while
Being defined
By who we are
And who we are not.

Part awakened...

At times
The most glorious,
Yet the most
Wayward of beings too.

Pranic Poetry

Believe in this place,
This charmed realm of ours.

For whilst
The heavens above
Play host
To variant voices,
Whatever still tumbles on
So freely down the hill
Is here for everyone of us,
My friend.

Dazzling proof,
Whatever the vagaries,
Of the future,
Or indeed
Follies of the past!
The core abundance,
The astonishing generosity
Of life remains.

And in the shape
Of many opportunities
Still to be mined...

Miracles out there
To be found.
To feel and witness,
To claim joyously
As our own.

The most telling
Of reminders
That despite
All our struggles
And self-doubt,
The seemingly endless
Huff and puff!

Deep, deep down
In our hearts,
We are pure enough.

Much as we first
Found ourselves,
Aren't we?

Pranic Poetry

Passing,
So often fruitlessly,
Through all the doors
To desire in life,
Far finer,
Faraway prizes
Twist and tease still,
Like runaway kites
Caught up
In a storm of being
That only
More stillness
Can becalm.

Oh, for an end
To such struggles!

And with kind
Devotion
Comes just that.

An embrace
Of perfect peace
That never fails
To usher in
Its own mysteriously
Unforeseen reward.

Blanket upon blanket
Of selflessness,
Nestled now securely
In the glowing casket
Of your soul.

Where, deep therein
Forever,
Lies the warmest
And truest of dividends.

The lingering presence
Of love
Beneath the fragile,
Needy contours of us all.

Pranic Poetry

Other titles of interest by Scott Hastie

All the publications listed below currently remain in print worldwide, as paperback editions and most also exist as ebooks. The exceptions being Scott's two earliest collections: Selected Poetry and New Poetry. Both of which are now due to be adapted for e-format in 2021.

Selected Poetry	ISBN: 978-0950977027
New Poetry	ISBN: 978-0950977034
Meditations	ISBN: 978-0950977058
Angel Voices	ISBN: 978-0950977072
Threads	ISBN: 978-0992709303
Pranic Poetry	ISBN: 978-0992709334
Splinters of Light *Quotations from the poetry* *of Scott Hastie*	ISBN: 978-0992709372

Printed in Poland
by Amazon Fulfillment
Poland Sp. z o.o., Wrocław